Parable of Community

Basic Texts of Taizé

by

Brother Roger of Taizé

MOWBRAY
LONDON & OXFORD

Copyright © Les Presses de Taizé 1980, 1984

ISBN 0 264 66732 8

This edition translated by Emily Chisholm and the Brothers
and first published in English 1980
by A. R. Mowbray & Co. Ltd
Saint Thomas House
Becket Street, Oxford, OX1 1SJ

Reprinted and updated 1984

Filmset by Northumberland Press Ltd,
Gateshead, Tyne and Wear
and printed in Great Britain by Richard Clay
(The Chaucer Press) Ltd, Bungay, Suffolk

The Rule of Taizé was first
published 1968 in French and English
by Les Presses de Taizé

PARABLE OF COMMUNITY

CONTENTS

PREFACE

Through visits, publications, and even the mass media, people in the English-speaking world are becoming more and more familiar with the Ecumenical Community of Taizé, located in the tiny village of that name in the heart of the Burgundy region of eastern France. But in order to understand the community's underlying vision, the best source by far are the texts which come from Taizé itself, and in which the brothers express in words their attempt to respond to Christ's call and their searching with young people all over the world. This volume presents four such writings, all by the community's founder and prior, Brother Roger.

The first of these texts – printed here in a new, up-to-date translation – was written around thirty years ago. During the winter of 1952–53, in the solitude of a long silent retreat, Brother Roger first put down on paper *The Rule of Taizé*. In it he expressed, for his brothers, 'the essential aspects of their common life.' He had already been living in Taizé for twelve years, alone for the first two and then in the company of his first brothers.

The following three texts date from much later. Beginning in the 1960s, young adults began coming to Taizé in ever greater numbers, and Brother Roger attempted to respond to their questions and preoccupations in a number of writings. The first of these letters was written in 1974 for the opening of the Council of Youth, which brought 40,000 people from throughout the world to the hill of Taizé. The final two texts were written in Africa and Latin America respectively, during visits in which Brother Roger and small groups of young people from every continent shared the lives and living conditions of some of the world's poorest people. Written in the same vein as *The Rule of Taizé*, they are meant for all, young and old, who are asking themselves what it means to live as a follower of Christ amidst the tensions and the struggles of the contemporary world.

THE RULE OF TAIZÉ

FOREWORD

Brother, if you submit to a common rule, you can only do so on account of Christ and the Gospel.[1]

From now on, your worship and your service are integrated in a brotherly community, itself set in the body of the Church. In the inner searching so necessary for your Christian life, you are stimulated by others' dynamism. You are not alone any more. Your brothers are to be reckoned with in everything.

So, far from groaning under the burden of a rule, rejoice: refusing to look back,[2] borne along with all by one and the same Word, every day you can once again hasten on towards Christ.

This rule contains the minimum needed for a community to grow up in Christ and devote itself to a common service of God. There is a risk implied in this resolve to set down only the essentials: your freedom might become a pretext for living according to your own impulses.

The sole grace of our Lord Jesus Christ assures you of salvation, so you have no disciplines to observe for their own sakes. The one aim of your search for self-mastery is greater availability. No pointless abstaining, keep to what God commands. Bear the burdens of others, accept whatever hurts each day brings, so that you are concretely in communion with the sufferings of Christ: there lies our main discipline.

You are afraid that a common rule may stifle your personality when its purpose is to free you from useless fetters, the better to bear responsibility and exercise all the boldness possible in your ministry.

You would restrict your understanding of the Gospel if you withheld some part of yourself for fear of losing your life. Unless the grain of wheat dies,[3] you cannot hope to see your life grow up and blossom into the fullness of Christian living.

Never stand still, advance with your brothers, race towards the goal in the steps of Christ. His path is a way of light – I am, but also, you are the light of the world[4] . . . For the light of Christ to penetrate you, it is not enough to contemplate it (as though you were purely spirit); you have to set out resolutely, body and soul, along that path.

Be a sign for others of joy and brotherly love.

Open yourself to all that is human and you will find that every vain desire to escape from the world disappears. Be present to your age; adapt yourself to the conditions of the moment. Father, I pray you, not to take them out of the world, but to keep them from evil.[5]

Love the deprived, all who are suffering man's injustice and thirsting for justice. Jesus had special concern for them. Never be afraid of their bothering you.

To your parents show deep affection; let its very quality help them to recognise the absolute nature of your vocation.

Love your neighbour, whatever his religious or ideological point of view.

Never resign yourself to the scandal of the separation of Christians, all so readily professing love for their neighbour, yet remaining divided. Make the unity of Christ's Body your passionate concern.

COMMON PRAYER

The disciples, full of great joy, met in the temple praising you,[6] and I too will tell all the wonders you have done; you have turned my mourning into gladness, you have girded me with joy, so my heart will sing your praise and not keep silent.[7]

Our common prayer is set within the communion of saints, but for this communion with the believers of every age to become a reality, we have to give ourselves to fervent intercession for mankind and the Church.

The Lord could do without our intercessions and our praise. Yet it is God's mystery that he demands of us, his fellow-workers, to keep on praying and never tire.[8]

Let us be careful to seek the inner meaning of liturgical actions and strive to perceive, in signs accessible to people of flesh and blood, an invisible reality pertaining to the Kingdom. But let us beware of multiplying these signs, being careful to preserve their simplicity – the token of their worth for the Gospel.

The liturgical vestment is worn to remind us that our whole being has been clothed by Christ. It is a way of expressing our praise of the Lord other than by words.

The praise of Christ expressed by the liturgy penetrates us insofar as it continues throughout the humblest tasks. In the regular rhythm of our common prayer, the love of Jesus grows in us, we do not know how.[9]

Common prayer does not dispense us from personal prayer. The one sustains the other. Let us take time each day to renew our personal intimacy with Jesus Christ.

In Christ's company we are filled beyond measure,[10] therefore let us surrender ourselves to the living Word of God, allowing it to reach the secret depths of our being and take possession not only of our minds but of our bodies as well.

Christ, the Word made flesh, gives himself to us visibly in the Sacrament. Draw strength from the Eucharist, the meal of thanksgiving, and never forget that it is offered to the sick among the People of God. It is for you, frail and weak as you always are.

There is no point in being upset during the common prayer if the brothers find it hard to keep together while singing. Certainly, the surrender of ourselves to a life hidden in Christ can never justify laziness or routine; it can only signify the active participation of our whole being, mind and body together.

If your attention wanders, return to prayer as soon as you realise the fact, without lamenting over it. Should you experience your weakness even in the very heart of the prayer, do not forget that in you the essential has already been accomplished.

There are days when the common prayer becomes a burden to you. Then simply offer your body; your presence is already proof of your desire, not realisable for the moment, to praise your Lord. Believe in Christ's presence within you, even if you can feel no apparent resonance.

MEALS

Every meal ought to be an agape overflow-ing with brotherly love, joy and simplicity of heart.[11]

The silence sometimes observed during a meal offers refreshment when you are tired, or communion in prayer for the companion who is sharing bread with you.

THE COUNCIL

The aim of the council is to seek all the light possible on the will of Christ for the ongoing life of the community. The first step is to bring yourself into silence, to be ready to listen to your Lord.

Nothing is more unfavourable to objective judgement than the ties of particular affinity; we may incline to support a brother in the perhaps unconscious hope of obtaining his support at some point in return. Nothing is more contrary to the spirit of the council than a search which has not been purified by the sole desire to discern God's will.

If there is one time when it is important to seek peace and pursue it,[12] avoid disputes and the temptation to prove yourself right, it is during the council.

Avoid a tone that precludes reply, the categorical 'we must'. Do not build up clever arguments to make yourself heard; express in a few words what you feel conforms most closely to God's plan, without imagining that you can impose it.

To avoid encouraging any spirit of rivalry, the prior is responsible before his Lord for making decisions without being bound by a majority. Set free from human pressures, he listens with the same attention to the most timid brother as to a brother full of self-assurance. If he senses a lack of real agreement on an important question, he should reserve judgement and, in order to advance, make a provisional decision, ready to review it later; standing still is disobedience for brothers advancing towards Christ. The prior knows best what each one is capable of; if a brother is to be given a responsibility, he is the first to propose it.

The council is composed of the brothers who have made profession; brothers who are absent are consulted by the prior or by a brother he has chosen.

HARMONY

Life in community is not possible without a minimum of harmony.

Why would you inconvenience your brothers by being late, or neglectful?

If some major reason demands your absence and you are unable to be present at an act of the community, do not excuse yourself through an intermediary.

Never be a hindrance by a lack of eagerness to return to the brothers with whom you have committed yourself totally, mind and body.

THROUGHOUT YOUR DAY
LET WORK AND REST
BE QUICKENED
BY THE WORD OF GOD

In your life of prayer and meditation look for the words God addresses to you, and put them into practice at once. So read little, but take your time over it.

If your praying is to be genuine, you need to be at grips with the demands of work. A careless or half-hearted attitude would make you incapable of true intercession. Strive for regularity in your work. Your prayer becomes total when it is one with your work.

Hour by hour pray, work or rest, but all in God.

In the work you do, never make comparisons between yourself and the other brothers. Your place is necessary for the witness of the whole community – in all simplicity, know how to keep it.

KEEP INNER SILENCE IN ALL THINGS AND YOU WILL DWELL IN CHRIST

Inner silence requires us first to forget our own selves and so quieten conflicting voices and master obsessive anxiety, constantly beginning again, never discouraged because always forgiven. It makes possible our conversation with Jesus Christ.

But who does not dread this silence, preferring to relax when it is time for work, then fleeing prayer and wearing himself out at useless jobs, neglecting his neighbour and himself?

Your dialogue with Christ demands this silence. Unless you keep offering him everything, and talk to him with the simplicity of a child, how will you find inner unity when by nature you are anxious or complacent?

You fear that this inner silence may leave some question within you unsettled? Then make a note of what is troubling you or causing resentment; the solution can be found later.

There are times when the silence of God in his creatures comes to a climax. Alone in retreat, we are renewed by the intimate encounter with Christ.

Peace and quiet are important for love of the brothers who are praying, reading, writing or, in the evening, resting.

Discretion in speech or gesture has never prevented human contact; only mute silence could cause relationships to break down. That is not required of us, because by itself it is not conducive to the true spirit of inner silence.

BE FILLED
WITH
THE SPIRIT OF
THE BEATITUDES:
JOY,
MERCY,
SIMPLICITY

JOY

In the communion of saints, day after day we sing the Lord's renewed compassion,[13] and his mercy kindles our fervour.

True joy begins within.

Acting the fool has never restored joy. Remember that there is no clear dividing-line between simple joking and the irony that demolishes. Mockery is cowardly because it serves to cloak so-called truths which nobody would dare to express in direct conversation.

Perfect joy lies in the utter simplicity of peaceful love. In order to shine out, such joy requires no less than your whole being.

Do not be afraid of sharing in others' trials, do not be afraid of suffering, for it is often in the depth of the abyss that we discover the perfection of joy in communion with Jesus Christ.

Perfect joy is self-giving. Whoever knows it seeks neither gratitude nor kindness. It is sheer wonder renewed by the sight of the generosity of the Giver of

all gifts, material and spiritual. It is
thankfulness. It is thanksgiving.

MERCY

As peace with Christ involves peace with your neighbour, seek reconciliation, make amends where you can.

Forgive your brother seventy times seven times.[14]

You may fear that a brother's pride will be flattered if you forget his offence: in that case exhort him, but only when the two of you are alone, and with the gentleness of Christ. If you refrain from doing so in order to safeguard your need of influence or popularity with certain brothers, you become an occasion of stumbling in the community.

Always be ready to forgive. Do not forget that love also finds expression in marks of mutual consideration. No weak sentimentality, and no harsh words. Consider when you speak impatiently how Christ is hurt.

Refuse to indulge in personal dislikes. They can easily flourish when the large number of brothers means that you cannot be open and free with everyone. Your natural inclinations may lead you to be prejudiced from the start, to judge your neighbour by his bad side. Let yourself be filled instead with an abundance of friendship for all.

Avoid petty disagreements between brothers. Nothing is more divisive than endless discussions about everything under the sun. See that you stop them when necessary. Refuse to listen to insinuations about a brother. Be a ferment of unity.

If you have doubts about a brother's attitude, and either you cannot talk to him about it or he refuses to listen to you, confide them to the prior and see together what can be done to help that brother. Should he then refuse to listen to you both, tell the community.[15]

Because of the weakness of your flesh, Christ offers you visible and repeated signs of his forgiveness. Absolution restores you to the joy of a reconciliation.[16] Still, you have to ask for it. The sin of one member marks the whole body, but God's forgiveness reintegrates into the community. Confession is made to one particular brother, chosen with the prior.

Anyone who lives in mercy is neither over-sensitive nor constantly disappointed. He gives himself simply, forgetting himself; joyfully, with all his heart; freely, not looking for anything in return.

SIMPLICITY

Availability means constantly simplifying your mode of living, not by constraint but by faith.

Flee the devious paths through which the tempter seeks you. Throw aside all useless burdens, the better to bring to Christ your Lord those of your fellow men.

In the transparency of brotherly love, admit your mistakes simply, never using them as a pretext for pointing out those of others. Wherever they are, brothers practise brief and frequent sharing together.

Simplicity is also loyalty towards oneself as a way of acquiring limpidity. It is a way of openness towards our neighbour.

Simplicity lies in the free joy of a brother who has given up any obsession with his own progress or backsliding to keep his eyes fixed on the light of Christ.

CELIBACY

Celibacy brings greater freedom to attend to the things of God,[17] but it can only be accepted with the aim of giving ourselves more completely to our neighbour with the love of Christ himself.

Our celibacy means neither indifference nor a break with human affections; it calls for their transfiguration. Christ alone can convert our passions into total love of our neighbour. When selfishness is not transcended by growing generosity, when you no longer resort to confession to overcome the need for self-assertion contained in every passion, when the heart is not constantly brimming over with great love, you can no longer let Christ love in you and your celibacy becomes a burden.

This working of Christ in you demands infinite patience.

Purity of heart is contrary to all natural tendencies.

Impurity, even in the imagination, leaves psychological traces which are not always removed instantly by confession and absolution. The main thing is to keep living new beginnings as a Christian never disheartened because always forgiven.

Purity of heart is closely linked with transparency. Do not display your difficulties, but do not withdraw either as though you were superhuman and exempt from struggles.

Refuse to connive in vulgarity. Certain jokes can revive the difficulties of brothers who are striving to remain pure in heart.

There is a slackness of attitude which could veil the true meaning of the difficult yet joyful commitment of chastity. Remember that your behaviour and your bearing are signs; neglect of them can hinder us on our way forward together.

Purity of heart can only be lived in spontaneous, joyful self-forgetting, as we give our lives for those we love.[18] Giving ourselves in this way means accepting that our susceptibilities will often be wounded.

There is no friendship without purifying suffering.

There is no love for our neighbour without the Cross. Only by the Cross can we know the unfathomable depths of love.

COMMUNITY OF GOODS

The pooling of goods is total.

The audacity involved in putting to good use all that is available at any time, not laying up capital and not fearing possible poverty, is a source of incalculable strength.

But if, like Israel, you save the bread from heaven for tomorrow,[19] you are in danger of pointlessly overstraining the brothers whose vocation is to live in the present.

Poverty has no virtue in itself.

The poor of the Gospel learn to live without having the next day's needs ensured, joyfully confident that everything will be provided.

The spirit of poverty does not mean looking poverty-stricken, but disposing everything in creation's simple beauty.

The spirit of poverty means living in the joyfulness of each present day. If for God there is the generosity of distributing all the good things of the earth, for man there is the grace of giving what he has received.

THE PRIOR, SERVANT OF COMMUNION

Without unity, there is no hope for bold and total service of Jesus Christ. Individualism breaks up the community and brings it to a halt.

The prior inspires unity within the community.

He points the way in matters of practical detail, but for every important question he listens to the council before making a decision.

The brothers should remain spontaneous with him; but remembering that the Lord has entrusted him with a charge, they should be attentive to all that concerns his ministry.

By their attitude of trust, the brothers renew the prior in the seriousness of his vocation for the joy of all; by their spirit of petty demands, they paralyze his ministry.

Each brother should frankly tell the prior, in private, the fears he may have. Revolt expressed before others is bound to contaminate, and it is here that the tempter finds his best weapons to divide what must remain one. Beware of childish reactions which accuse others when it would be more appropriate first to accuse ourselves.

The spirit of perfection, if that means imposing one's own point of view as the best, is a scourge in the community. True perfection, precisely, is bearing the imperfections of our neighbour, for sheer love.

The prior is subject to the same failings as his brothers. If they love him for his human qualities, they risk no longer accepting him in his ministry when they discover his faults.

The prior appoints a brother to ensure continuity after him.

Making decisions is a formidable task for the prior.

He should keep alert and pray so as to build up the whole body in Christ.

He should look for the special gifts of each brother, so that the brother can discern them for himself.

He should not consider his charge to be superior, nor must he assume it in a spirit of resignation. He should bear in mind only that it has been entrusted to him by Christ, to whom he will have to give account.

He should root out all authoritarianism in himself, but never be weak, in order to maintain his brothers in God's plan. He should prevent the authoritarian from dominating and give confidence to the weak.

He should arm himself with mercy and ask Christ to grant it as the grace most essential for him.

BROTHERS ON MISSION

Like the disciples sent out two by two,[20] brothers on mission are witnesses to Christ, called to be a sign of his presence among all and bearers of joy.

Everywhere and at all times, they represent the community; the witness of the whole body depends on their attitude. They keep the prior regularly informed about their life. They should not venture into any new project without his agreement, as he is responsible for consulting others. If brothers on mission fail to keep this close contact, they very soon break the unity of the body.

If they are two or more, the prior designates one of them to be in charge.

Their spiritual life is that of the community.

NEW BROTHERS

To prepare himself to follow Christ, each new brother requires time to mature.

He should beware of the illusion that he has now arrived. Even if he assimilates rapidly, he needs time to understand the vocation in its utmost consequences.

As long as we are not known by new brothers, we are tempted to monopolise them for ourselves. We should remember that there are brothers appointed to listen to them and to prepare them for profession.

GUESTS

In each guest it is Christ himself whom we have to receive; so let us learn to be welcoming and be ready to offer our free time. Our hospitality should be generous and discerning.

During meals the brothers should be attentive to the presence of a guest and be careful not to disconcert him.

Certain brothers are responsible for the welcome while other brothers continue with their work. This helps to avoid dilettantism.

CONCLUSION

There is a danger in having indicated with this rule only the essentials for a common life. Better run this risk, and not settle into complacency and routine.

If this rule were ever to be regarded as an end in itself, dispensing us from always searching to discover more of God's plan, more of the love of Christ, more of the light of the Holy Spirit, we would be laying a useless burden on our shoulders: better then never to have written it.

If Christ is to grow in me, I must know my own weakness and that of my brothers. For them I will become all things to all, and give even my life, for Christ's sake and the Gospel's.[21]

EXHORTATION READ AT PROFESSION

Brother, what do you ask?

The mercy of God and the community of my brothers.

May God complete in you what he has begun.

Brother, you trust in God's mercy: remember that the Lord Christ comes to help the weakness of your faith; committing himself with you, he fulfils for you his promise:

'Truly, there is no one who has given up home, brothers, sisters, mother, father, wife or children for my sake and the Gospel's, who will not receive a hundred times as much at present – homes and brothers and sisters and mothers and children – and persecutions too, and in the age to come eternal life.'[22]

This is a way contrary to all human reason; like Abraham you can only advance along it by faith, not by sight,[23] always sure that whoever loses his life for Christ's sake will find it.[24]

From now on walk in the steps of Christ. Do not be anxious about tomorrow.[25] First seek God's Kingdom and its justice.[26] Surrender yourself, give yourself, and good measure, pressed down, shaken together, brimming over, will be poured out for you; the measure you give is the measure you will receive.[27]

Whether you wake or sleep, night and day the seed springs up and grows, you do not know how.[28]

Avoid parading your goodness before people to gain their admiration.[29] Never let your inner life make you look sad, like a hypocrite who puts on a grief-stricken air to attract attention. Anoint your head and wash your face, so that only your Father who is in secret knows what your heart intends.[30]

Stay simple and full of joy, the joy of the merciful, the joy of brotherly love.

Be vigilant. If you have to rebuke a brother, keep it between the two of you.[31]

Be concerned to establish communion with your neighbour.

Be open about yourself, remembering that you have a brother whose charge it is to listen to you. Bring him your understanding so that he can fulfil his ministry with joy.[32]

The Lord Christ, in his compassion and his love for you, has chosen you to be in the Church a sign of brotherly love. It is his will that with your brothers you live the parable of community.

So, refusing to look back,[33] and joyful with infinite gratitude, never fear to outstrip the dawn,[34]

praising
blessing
and singing
Christ your Lord.

THE COMMITMENTS
MADE AT
PROFESSION

Receive me, Lord, and I will live;
may my expectation be a source of joy.

Brother, remember that it is Christ who
calls you and that it is to him that you are
now going to respond.

Will you, for love of Christ, consecrate
yourself to him with all your being?
  I will.
Will you henceforth fulfil your service of
God within our community, in communion with your brothers?
  I will.
Will you, renouncing all ownership, live
with your brothers not only in community of material goods but also in
community of spiritual goods, striving
for openness of heart?
  I will.
Will you, in order to be more available to
serve with your brothers, and in order to

give yourself in undivided love to Christ, remain in celibacy?

I will.

Will you, so that we may be of one heart and one mind and so that the unity of our common service may be fully achieved, adopt the orientations of the community expressed by the prior, bearing in mind that he is only a poor servant of communion in the community?

I will.

Will you, always discerning Christ in your brothers, watch over them in good days and bad, in suffering and in joy?

I will.

In consequence, because of Christ and the Gospel, you are henceforth a brother of our community.

PRAYER

Lord Christ, gentle and humble of heart,
we hear your timid call:
'You, follow me.'
You give us this vocation
so that together we may live a parable of
communion and, having taken the risk of an
entire lifetime, we may be ferments of
reconciliation in that irreplaceable
communion called the Church.
Show us how to respond courageously,
without getting trapped
in the quicksand of our hesitations.
Come, so that we may be sustained
by the breath of your Spirit,
the one thing that matters,
without which nothing impels us
to keep on moving forward.
You ask all who know
how to love and suffer with you
to leave themselves behind and follow you.
When, to love with you and not without you,
we must abandon some project contrary to your
plan, then come, O Christ,
and fill us with quiet confidence:
make us realise that your love
will never disappear,
and that to follow you means giving our lives.

A LIFE
WE NEVER DARED HOPE FOR

The following letter has also been published at the end
of the third volume of Brother Roger's journal
(1972–74), likewise entitled *A Life We Never Dared
Hope For*.

I know you want to fashion your life in communion with Christ who is love, so I have written this letter for you. You will feel freer to move from one provisional stage to the next, if you rely throughout your life on a small number of essential values — a few simple truths.

HE LOVED YOU FIRST

Together with the whole people of God, with people from all over the world, you are invited to live a life exceeding all your hopes. On your own, how could you ever experience the radiance of God's presence?

God is too dazzling to be looked upon. He is a God who blinds our sight. It is Christ who channels this consuming fire, and allows God to shine through without dazzling us.

Christ is present, close to each one of us, whether we know him or not. He is so bound up with us that he lives within us, even when we are unaware of him. He is there in secret, a fire burning in the heart, a light in the darkness.

But Christ is also someone other than yourself. He is alive; he stands beyond, ahead of you.

Here is his secret: he loved you first.

That is the meaning of your life: to be loved for ever, loved to all eternity, so that you, in turn, will dare to give your life. Without love, what is the point of living?

From now on, in prayer or in struggle, only one thing is disastrous, the loss of love. Without love, what is the good of believing, or even of giving your body to the flames?

Do you see? Contemplation and struggle arise from the very same source, Christ who is love.

If you pray, it is out of love. If you struggle to restore dignity to the exploited, that too is for love.

Will you agree to set out on this road? At the risk of losing your life for love, will you live Christ for others?

WITH PEOPLE ALL OVER THE WORLD

On our own, what can we do to give the voiceless their say, and to promote a society without castes?

With the whole People of God, collectively, it is possible to light a fire on the earth.

One of Christ's questions hits home. When that poor person was hungry, did you recognise me in him? Where were you when I was sharing the life of the utterly destitute? Have you been the oppressor of even one single human being? When I said 'Woe to the rich' – rich in money, or rich in dogmatic certainties – did you prefer the illusions of wealth?

Your struggle cannot be lived out in ideas that fly from pillar to post and never become reality.

Free from oppression the poor and the exploited, and to your astonishment you will see signs of resurrection springing up, here and now.

Share all you have for greater justice.

Make no one your victim. Brother to all, a universal brother, run to whoever is despised and rejected.

'Love those who hate you. Pray for those who wrong you.' In hatred, how could you reflect anything of Christ? 'Love your neighbour as yourself.' If you hated yourself, what damage that would do!

But as your life has been filled to overflowing, you try to understand everything in others.

The closer you come to communion, the more efforts the tempter will make. To be free of him, sing Christ until you are joyful and serene.

Tensions can be creative. But when your relationship with someone has deteriorated into seething inner contradictions and non-communication, remember that beyond the desert something else lies waiting.

We judge other people by what we are ourselves, by our own hearts. Remember only the best you have found in others. With words of liberation on your lips, not a mouthful of condemnation, do not waste your energy looking at the speck in your brother's eye.

If you suffer unfair criticism for the sake of Christ, dance and forgive as God has forgiven. You will find that you are free, free beyond compare.

In any disagreement, what is the point of trying to find out who was right and who was wrong?

Have nothing to do with clever diplomacy; aim at transparency of heart; never manipulate another's conscience, using his anxiety as a lever to force him into your scheme of things.

In every domain, when things are too easy creativity is low. Poverty of means leads to living intensely, in the joy of the present moment. But joy vanishes if poverty of means leads to austerity or to judging others.

Poverty of means gives birth to a sense of the universal. And the festival begins once more. The festival will never end.

If festival disappeared from mankind... If we were to wake up, one fine morning, in a society replete but emptied of all spontaneity... If praying became mere words, so secularised that it lost all sense of mystery, leaving no room for the prayer of gesture and posture, for poetry, for emotion or for intuition . . . If we were to lose childlike trust in the Eucharist and the Word of God . . . If, on our grey days, we were to demolish all we had grasped on days of light . . . If we were to decline the joy offered by Him who eight times over declares 'Happy' (Matthew 5).

If festival disappears from the Body of Christ, if the Church is a place of retrenchment and not of universal comprehension, in all the world where could we find a place of friendship for the whole of humanity?

WE ARE OURSELVES ONLY IN GOD'S PRESENCE

If you feel no sense of God's presence within you when you pray, why worry? There is no precise dividing-line between emptiness and fullness, any more than between doubt and faith, or fear and love.

The essential is always concealed from your own eyes. But that only makes you more eager than ever to progress towards the one reality. Then, gradually, it becomes possible to sense something of the depth and the breadth of a love beyond all comprehension. At that point you touch the gates of contemplation, and there you draw the energy you need for new beginnings, for daring commitments.

Discovering what kind of person you are, with nobody there to understand you, can provoke a sense of shame at being alive, strong enough to lead to self-destruction. At times it makes you feel that you are living under sentence. But, for the Gospel, there is neither 'normal' nor 'abnormal', only human beings, made in the image of God. Then who could condemn? Jesus prays in you. He offers the liberation of forgiveness to all who live in poverty of heart, so that they, in their turn, may become liberators of others.

In every single one of us there is a place of solitude no human relationship can fill, not even the deepest love between two individuals. Anyone who does not accept this solitude sooner or later revolts against other people, and against God himself.

And yet you are never alone. Let yourself be plumbed to the depths, and you will realise that everyone is created for a presence. There, in your heart of hearts, in that place where no two people are alike, Christ is waiting for you. And there the unexpected happens.

In a flash, the love of God, the Holy Spirit, streaks through each one of us like lightning in our night. The risen Christ takes hold of you, and he takes over. He takes upon himself everything that is unbearable. It is only later, sometimes much later, that you realise: Christ came, he gave his overflowing life.

The moment your eyes are opened you will say, 'My heart was burning within me as he spoke.'

Christ does not destroy flesh and blood. In communion with him there is no room for alienation. He does not break what is in us. He has not come to destroy, but to fulfil. When you listen, in the silence of your heart, he transfigures all that troubles you most. When you are shrouded in what you cannot understand, when darkness gathers, his love is a flame. You need only fix your gaze on that lamp burning in the darkness, till day begins to dawn and the sun rises in your heart.

HAPPY ARE THEY WHO DIE FOR LOVE

Never a pause, O Christ, in your persistent questioning: 'Who do you say that I am?'

You are the one who loves me into endless life.

You open up the way of risk. You go ahead of me along the way of holiness, where happy are they who die of love, where the ultimate response is martyrdom.

Day by day you transfigure the 'No' in me into 'Yes'. You ask me, not for a few scraps, but for the whole of my existence.

You are the one who prays in me day and night. My stammerings are prayer: simply calling you by your name, Jesus, fills our communion to the full.

You are the one who, every morning, slips on my finger the ring of the prodigal son, the ring of festival.

So why have I wavered so long? Have I 'exchanged the glory of God for something useless; have I left the spring of

living water to build myself cracked cis-
terns that hold nothing?' (Jeremiah 2)

You have been seeking me unweary-
ingly. Why did I hesitate once again,
asking for time to deal with my own
affairs? Once I had set my hand to the
plough, why did I look back? Without
realising it, I was making myself unfit to
follow you.

Yet, though I had never seen you, I
loved you.

You kept on saying: live the little bit of
the Gospel you have grasped. Proclaim
my life. Light fire on the earth... You,
follow me...

Until one day I understood: you were
asking me to commit myself to the point of
no return.

PRAYER

You are the God of every human being
and, too dazzling to be looked at,
you let yourself be seen as in a mirror,
shining on the face of Christ.
We are eager
to glimpse a reflection of your presence
in the obscurity of persons and events –
so open in us the gates of transparency
of
heart.
In that portion of solitude
which is the lot of every one,
come and refresh
the dry and thirsty ground of our body
and our spirit.
Come and place a spring of living water
in the lifeless regions of our being.
Come and bathe us in your confidence
to make even our inner deserts
burst into flower.

THE WONDER OF A LOVE

The following letter has also been published at the end
of the fourth volume of Brother Roger's journal
(1974–76), likewise entitled *The Wonder of a Love*.

*You are seeking fulfilment, so from Africa I
am writing you this letter. It is the sequel to
another letter, 'A Life We Never Dared
Hope For'.*

HE NEVER FORCES ANYONE'S HAND

You keep on asking me, 'How can I find fulfilment?'

If only I could lay my hand on your shoulder and go with you along the way.

Both of us together, turning towards Him who, recognised or not, is your quiet companion, someone who never imposes himself.

Will you let him plant a source of refreshment deep within you? Or will you be so filled with shame that you say, 'I am not good enough to have you near me?'

What fascinates in God is his humility. He never punishes, never domineers nor wounds human dignity. Any authoritarian gesture on our part disfigures his face and repels.

As for Christ, 'poor and humble of heart', – he never forces anyone's hand.

If he forced himself upon you, I would not be inviting you to follow him.

In the silence of the heart, tirelessly he whispers to each of us, 'Don't be afraid; I am here.'

DYING AND RISING WITH JESUS

To joy he calls us, not to gloom.

No groaning at the bonds that bind you, or the tyranny of a self you want to preserve. No drawing back into yourself, intent on mere survival, but at every stage in life, a new birth.

His joy not for your private possession, or all happiness would flee.

I would like to help you make your life a poem of love with him. Not a facile poem, but through the very greyness of your days, his joyfulness, even hilarity. Without them, how could there be fulfilment?

Whatever your doubts or your faith, he has already placed ahead of you what fires your enthusiasm.

Nobody can answer for you. You and you alone must dare.

But how?

Go to the ends of the earth and plunge into the conditions of those society rejects; overturn the powers of injustice; restore human dignity: is that taking risks? Yes, but that's not all there is to life.

Or again: sharing all you own, could that be the risk of the Gospel?

As you try to follow Christ, the day will come when you are irresistibly drawn to that. Responding will mean drinking deep at the unfailing springs. Anyone refusing to quench his thirst there first would become, unconsciously, a doctrinaire of sharing.

But what is the greatest risk to which this Man of humble heart invites everyone? It is 'dying and rising with Jesus.'

Passing with him from death to life; at times accompanying him in his agony for all the human family and, each day anew, beginning to rise from the dead with him.

Joyful, not overwhelmed. Every moment, leaving everything with him, even your weary body. And using no exotic methods, for then you would have lost the sense of praying.

Will you be able to wait for him when your heart cries out in loneliness, and the ultimate question is torn from your soul, 'But where is God?'

Wait for him, even when body and spirit are dry and parched. Wait, too, with many others for an event to occur in man's present day. An event which is neither marvel nor myth, nor a projection of yourself. The fruit of prayerful waiting, it comes concretely in the wake of a miracle from God.

In prayer, prayer that is always poor, like lightning rending the night, you will discover his secret: you can find fulfilment only in the presence of God ... and also, you will awaken others to God, first and foremost, by the life you live.

With burning patience, don't worry that you can't pray well. Surely you know that any spiritual pretension is death to the soul before you begin.

Even when you cannot recognise him, will you stay close to him in long silences when nothing seems to be happening? There, with him, life's most significant decisions take shape. There the recurring 'what's the use?' and the scepticism of the disillusioned melt away.

Tell him everything, and let him sing within you the radiant gift of life. Tell him everything, even what cannot be expressed and what is absurd.

When you understand so little of his language, talk to him about it.

In your struggles, he brings a few words, an intuition or an image to your mind... And within you grows a desert flower, a flower of delight.

THE FIRE OF HIS FORGIVENESS

Fulfilment? I would like to clear you a path to the springs of living water. There and nowhere else, imagination and the potent energies of risk blossom and flourish.

Don't you see? In every human being, a gift that is unique. Everything exists to a greater or lesser degree within you, every possible tendency. In you fertile fields, in you scorched deserts.

Fulfilment? Don't count yourself among those who have made it. You would lose vital energies, and the transfiguration of the will into creative potential.

No self-indulgence. Don't waste time in dead-end situations. Move on, unhesitating, to the essential step, and quickly.

Unconsciously, you may wound what you touch. Only Christ can touch without wounding.

Consider your neighbour not just in one stage of his life, but in all its phases. So don't try to separate the weeds from the wheat. You will only uproot them both and leave devastation behind you, exchanging the gleaming pearl for cracked earth that cannot hold water.

But you say, 'How can I fulfil myself when there is an image from my past which covers the spring of living water in ashes? . . . Forget the ravages of the past? Nobody can do that; nor the still throbbing pangs of clinging regret.'

But let just one sigh rise from deep within you, and already you are overflowing with confidence. What holds you in its clutches is being dealt with by God.

For you, this prayer: 'Forgive them, they don't know what they are doing; forgive me, I didn't know what I was doing.'

'Love!' It's easily said. Forgiving means loving to the utmost . . . Forgive not in order to change the other person but solely to follow Christ. No one can come closer to the living God than that . . . And you yourself become a source of forgiveness.

In times of darkness, when life loses its meaning and you are unsure even of your own identity, a flame still burns bright enough to lighten your night . . .

... The fire of his forgiveness plunges deep within you, dispelling your own confusion; he calls you by your name; and the fire burns away your bitterness to its very roots. That fire never says 'enough.'

BECOME WHAT YOU ARE

Fulfilment? Could you be hesitating over a choice for fear of making a mistake? Bogged down perhaps in the mire of indecision?

The fact is, a yes to Christ for life is surrounded by an element of error; but this is already purified, from the start, by an act of faith. So set out unseeing, taking him at his word.

Don't summon your own darkness again to cover your refusal. Happy all who tear their hand from their eyes to take the greatest of all risks, 'dying and rising with Christ.'

Fulfilment? Become what you are in your heart of hearts.

. . . and the gates of childhood will open, the wonder of a love.

PRAYER

Breath of Christ's loving,
flood over all who experience fears or little
deaths; breathe your resurrection
into our very minds, our very flesh.
Happy are they who take the greatest of all
risks and live a passover with Christ.
Yes, keeping close to you,
Jesus our joy,
in your agony for us all
and also in your resurrection.
Happy whoever tears his hand from his eyes
and no longer calls upon his darkness
to cover his refusal.
O Christ, you know that,
without intending to,
when we touch our neighbour
we sometimes wound.
While your touch never wounds
and tirelessly you remind us:
'Don't be afraid; I am here.'

ITINERARY FOR A PILGRIM

To struggle with a reconciled heart

This text was written in Latin America with a group of young people. It forms part of a 'Letter to All Communities.'

CELEBRATE THE MOMENT WITH GOD

Without looking back, you want to follow Christ: here and now, in the present moment, turn to God and trust in the Gospel. In so doing, you draw from the sources of jubilation.

You think you do not know how to pray. Yet the Risen Christ is there; he loves you before you love him. By 'his Spirit who dwells in our hearts', he intercedes in you far more than you imagine.

Even without recognising him, learn to wait for him with or without words, during long silences when nothing seems to happen. There obsessive discouragements vanish, creative impulses well up. Nothing can be built up in you without this adventure – finding him in the intimacy of a personal encounter. No one can do it for you.

When you have trouble understanding what he wants of you, tell him so. In the course of daily activities, at every moment, tell him all, even things you cannot bear.

Do not compare yourself with others, and with what they can do. Why wear yourself out regretting what is impossible for you? Could you have forgotten God? Turn to him. No matter what happens, dare to begin over and over again.

If you were to accuse yourself of all that is in you, your days and nights would not suffice. You have something better to do: in the present moment, celebrate God's forgiveness, despite the resistances to believing yourself forgiven, whether by God or by others.

When inner trials or incomprehensions from without make themselves felt, remember that in the very same wound where the poison of anxiety festers, there too the energies for loving are born.

If you seem to be walking in a thick fog, waiting for him, Christ, means giving him the time to put everything in its place . . . A fountain of gladness will spring up in the desert of your heart. Not a euphoric bliss, not just any kind of joy, but that jubilation which comes straight from the wellsprings of Eternity.

STRUGGLE WITH A RECONCILED HEART

Without looking back, you want to follow Christ: be prepared, in a life of great simplicity, to struggle with a reconciled heart.

Wherever you are placed, do not be afraid of the struggle for the oppressed, whether believers or not. The search for justice calls for a life of concrete solidarity with the very poorest . . . words alone can become a drug.

Prepare yourself as well, whatever the cost, for that struggle within yourself to remain faithful to Christ until death. This continuity of an entire lifetime will create in you an inner unity enabling you to pass through anything.

Struggling with a reconciled heart means being able to stand firm in the midst of crippling tensions. Far from smothering your energies, this struggle calls upon you to gather together all your vital forces.

Your intentions will perhaps be distorted. If you remain unforgiving, if you refuse a reconciliation, what do you reflect of Christ? Without a prayer for your opponent, what darkness within you! If you lose the ability to forgive, you have lost everything.

Alone, you cannot do much for others. Together, in community, animated by the breath of Christ's loving, a way forward opens up leading from aridity to a common creation. And when a community is a ferment of reconciliation in that communion which is the Church, then the impossible becomes possible.

You try to be leaven in the dough, you try to love the Church, and so often you come up against internal divisions that tear apart Christ's Body, his Church. What characterises those who seek reconciliation is that, following Christ, they wish to fulfill more than to destroy, to understand more than to exhort. At all times they remain within, until the very fragilities of the Church are transfigured.

When divisions and rivalries bring things to a standstill, nothing is more important than setting out to visit and listen to one another, and to celebrate the paschal mystery together.

When you are afraid of being criticised, in order to protect yourself, spontaneously you may react by taking the initiative and criticising first. Would you make use of the weapon of a guilty conscience, so contrary to the Gospel, to get something from another? Try to understand others with that all-important trust which comes from the heart; the intelligence will catch up later.

Far from lighting short-lived blazes, give your life to the end, and day after day it will become a creation with God. The further you advance in a communion with Christ, the more you are led to find concrete steps to take in your daily life.

ACCOMPANY CHRIST BY A
SIMPLE LIFE

Without looking back, you want to follow
Christ: remember that you cannot walk in
Christ's footsteps and at the same time
follow yourself. He is the way, a way
leading you irresistibly to a simple life, a
life of sharing.

The Gospel calls you to leave all things
behind. But leaving yourself behind is not
a matter of self-destruction; it means
choosing God as your first love.
Simplifying and sharing does not entail
opting for austerity or that self-sufficiency
which is a burden on others. Nor does it
mean glorifying a harsh and abject
poverty.

Simplify in order to live intensely, in
the present moment: you will discover the
joy of being alive, so closely linked to joy
in the living God. Simplify and share as a
way of identifying with Christ Jesus, born
poor among the poor.

If simplifying your existence were to
awaken a guilty conscience because of all

you can never achieve, then stop and take the time to think things over: jubilation, not groaning; everything around you should be festive. Use your imagination in arranging the little you have, to bring gaiety to the monotony of your days.

You need so little to live, so little to welcome others. When you open your home, too many possessions are a hindrance rather than a help to communion with others. Wearing yourself out to ensure an easy life for members of your family risks placing them in a relationship of dependence.

Do not worry if you have very little to share – such weak faith, so few belongings. In the sharing of this little, God fills you to overflowing, inexhaustibly.

PRAYER

O Christ,
in every creature you place
first and for ever a word:
God's forgiveness and his confidence in us.
To walk in your footsteps
you offer us the energy always to begin anew.
Following you
through the humble events of every day
means discerning a way –
not a law burdening us with obligations,
but you, O Christ, you are the Way
and on this road God comes to meet us.

ABOUT THE TAIZÉ COMMUNITY

ABOUT THE TAIZÉ COMMUNITY

Taizé is the name of a tiny village hidden away in the hills of Burgundy, in the eastern part of France, not far from the town of Cluny. Since 1940 it is also the home of an ecumenical community of brothers whose prayer, three times each day, is at the centre of their life. Finally, today Taizé is a place to which visitors of all ages and backgrounds come on pilgrimage, and to participate in international meetings of prayer and reflection.

Brother Roger first came to the village of Taizé in 1940, at the age of twenty-five. He dreamt of starting a community 'on account of Christ and the Gospel', and he chose to do so in an area in those years strongly marked by human distress. It was wartime, and his house became a place of welcome for refugees, especially Jews, fleeing from the Nazi occupation. After living alone for two years he was joined by his first brothers, and in 1949, when there were seven of them, together they committed themselves for life to celibacy and to life together. Year after year, other brothers make the same monastic commitments.

At first, the community was made up of brothers from different Protestant denominations. Today it includes many Catholics as well. By its very nature Taizé is an ecumenical community. It is also international: its eighty or so brothers come from some twenty different countries throughout the world. All the brothers do not always remain in Taizé; some live in small groups, known as fraternities, among the poor on different continents. Since 1966, members of an international Catholic congregation of sisters, who live according to the spirit of St Ignatius of Loyola, have taken responsibility for a large part of the work of welcoming people to Taizé; their house is located in a nearby village.

Taizé's vocation is to strive for communion among all. From its beginnings, the community has worked for reconciliation among Christians split apart into different denominations. But the brothers do not view reconciliation among Christians as an end in itself: it concerns all of humanity, since it makes the Church a place of communion for all.

During the first twenty years of its existence, the community lived in relative isolation. Then, gradually, young people between the ages of 18 and 30 began coming to Taizé, in ever-increasing numbers. Out of this grew the idea of holding a 'Council of Youth.' Announced in 1970, opened at Taizé in 1974 with 40,000 people present, for years it has involved people from all over the world in a common search.

In Taizé itself this search takes place during the international meetings which bring young people from many different countries to the hill throughout much of the year. Participants enter into the prayer of the community, and share their lives and concerns with one another; they look for ways of living lives of prayer and commitment in their own local situations. Others come to Taizé to confront their lives with the Gospel in the solitude of a silent retreat.

But this search is not limited to the hill of Taizé. Through meetings and visits it spreads out to many countries and continents. From time to time, too, letters are written by the young people to allow others as well to reflect on the questions and topics which are so crucial for them.

In 1974, for example, a group of young people from every continent drafted a *First Letter to the People of God,* which called upon Christians to be at one and the same time 'a contemplative people, thirsting for God; a people of justice, living the struggle of the exploited; a people of communion, where the non-believer also finds a creative place.' On the same occasion, Brother Roger wrote the personal letter entitled *A Life We Never Dared Hope For*.

A *Second Letter to the People of God* was written in 1976 by Brother Roger and another inter-continental group of young people at Calcutta, during a stay of several weeks there among the poorest of the poor. As a contribution to a different future for all, says the letter, 'the People of God can build up a parable of sharing in the human family.' The letter goes on to discuss some con-crete ways of sharing, and more concrete sugges-tions were proposed the following year in a *Letter to All Generations*, written on the South China Sea amidst people living on junks in the water.

The *Acts of the Council of Youth 1979* were written in one of the worst slums of Africa, Kenya's Mathare Valley, where Brother Roger wrote the letter, *The Wonder of a Love;* the texts were made public during a 'European meeting' which brought 15,000 people to Paris in December 1978. These *Acts* announce the end of a winter, a springtime of the Church. They make a number of concrete suggestions, urging people among other things to take an active part in the life of local Christian communities, parishes and congregations. The Council of Youth in fact has never wished to be a 'movement' apart, organised around Taizé, but rather a current of communion stimulating everyone to become more committed in their own particular situation.

To sum up four years of searching among the poor and outcast, Brother Roger and a group of young people wrote a *Letter to All Communities*. They prepared it in late 1979 while sharing the life of a poor district of Temuco, in the south of Chile. The letter is addressed both to 'small provisional communities' and to 'parishes and congregations, those large communities at the "base" of the Church'. It calls them to leave behind passivity, discouragement, and rivalries, to enter into a 'common creation' with a 'preferential option for the poor and the young.' And since no one can take part in a creation with others without beginning a personal creation within themselves, the letter includes the *Itinerary for a Pilgrim*, to help everyone to set out and follow Christ. These texts were made public during a European meeting held in Barcelona.

As a concrete means of undertaking this 'common creation', people both young and old have begun small pilgrimages in many different places. They are like rivulets of prayer and communion flowing into a larger river, a 'worldwide pilgrimage of reconciliation' opened by Brother Roger in Lebanon on Christmas Day 1982.

This worldwide pilgrimage includes 'stations' in different countries. At the end of 1980 and 1982, two large European meetings were held in the parishes of Rome, both times with a prayer service in St Peter's involving Pope John Paul II. In 1981, over fifteen thousand young Europeans crossed the Channel in a single night to join their British counterparts for a European meeting in London. Participants filled Westminster Abbey, Westminster Cathedral and St Paul's Cathedral, wired together for sound. In late 1983, Brother Roger joined young people for a European meeting in Paris after returning from several weeks spent among the poorest of the poor in Haiti and the Dominican Republic. As part of the pilgrimage, world gatherings, beginning 1985, are being prepared throughout all the continents.

TO LEARN MORE ABOUT TAIZÉ

TO LEARN MORE ABOUT TAIZÉ

1. THE WRITINGS OF BROTHER ROGER
   Living Today for God
   Dynamic of the Provisional
   Violent for Peace
   Brother Roger's journal:
     1. *Festival without End* (1969–70)
     2. *Struggle and Contemplation*
        (1970–72)
     3. *A Life We Never Dared Hope For*
        (1972–74)
     4. *The Wonder of a Love* (1974–76)
     5. *And Your Deserts Shall Flower*
        (1977–79)
   All published by Mowbray of Oxford.

2. OTHER WRITINGS
   The Story of Taizé by J.-L. G. Balado
   (Mowbray).
   Taizé – trust, forgiveness, reconciliation
   (Mowbray: colour photographs and
   short texts by Brother Roger. A set of 36
   slides and a tape cassette are available in
   conjunction with this booklet.)

3. PRAYER AT TAIZÉ
   *Praise in All Our Days, Common Prayer at
   Taizé* (Mowbray). Published in the USA
   by Oxford University Press under the
   title *Praise God*.
   Praise: Prayers from Taizé (shorter version
   of above book, published by Mowbray).
   Psalms for Praise from Taizé (Mowbray:

original, modern translation of the Psalms).

Praying together in word and song (Mowbray; G.I.A. Publications in USA. Suggestions for common prayer including readings, chants, prayers by Brother Roger.)

Music from Taizé (Collins Liturgical Publications; G.I.A. Publications in USA. Music by Jacques Berthier. Vocal and instrumental editions available.)

Chants nouveaux (Les Presses de Taizé. Songs in different languages, including English. Vocal and instrumental editions.)

4. PERIODICALS

The *Letter from Taizé*, a monthly newsletter published in eight languages (including English), gives news of young people and their searching on every continent, publishes prayers and texts for meditation. A yearly subscription to the English edition costs £4.50 (UK); $9.00 (USA); 50 crowns (Sweden), $10 (Australia), $13 (NZ), including airmail postage to all countries. Subscriptions can be obtained by writing to Taizé.

5. RECORDS AND CASSETTES

Louange des jours (Common prayer at Taizé) (Taizé 3001).

Canons and Litanies (Taizé 3004 and cassette TZ 404).

Cantate! (Taizé 3005 and cassette TZ 405).

Chanter ensemble (cassette TZ 452).

Distribution: AUVIDIS, Paris, or write to Taizé.
Address: 71250 Taizé-Community, France
Telephone: (85) 50.14.14
Telex: COTAIZE 800753-F

NOTES

1. Mark 10.29
2. Philippians 3.13
3. John 12.24
4. John 8.12 and Matthew 5.14
5. John 17.15
6. Luke 24.53
7. Psalm 30. 11–12
8. Luke 18.1
9. Mark 4.27
10. Luke 6.38
11. Acts 2.46
12. Psalm 34.14
13. Lamentations 3.22–23
14. Matthew 18.22
15. Matthew 18.17
16. Psalm 51. 12
17. See 1 Corinthians 7.32
18. John 15.13
19. See Exodus 16
20. Luke 10.1
21. Mark 10.29
22. Mark 10.29–30 and Luke 18.29–30
23. 2 Corinthians 5.7
24. Matthew 16.25
25. Matthew 6.34
26. Matthew 6.33
27. Luke 6.38
28. Mark 4.27
29. Matthew 6.1
30. Matthew 6.16–18
31. Matthew 18.15
32. Hebrews 13.17
33. Philippians 3.13
34. Psalm 119.147